P9-DFU-124

EDGE BOOKS™

WEAPONS, GEAR, AND UNIFORMS
✳ OF THE ✳
IRAQ WAR

by Shelley Tougas

Consultant:
Jennifer L. Jones
Chair, Armed Forces History
NMAH, Smithsonian Institution
Washington, D.C.

CAPSTONE PRESS
a capstone imprint

Edge Books are published by Capstone Press,
1710 Roe Crest Drive, North Mankato, Minnesota 56003.
www.capstonepub.com

Books published by Capstone Press are manufactured with paper
containing at least 10 percent post-consumer waste.

Library of Congress Cataloging-in-Publication Data
Tougas, Shelley.
    Weapons, gear, and uniforms of the Iraq War / by Shelley Tougas.
    p. cm.—(Edge books. Equipped for battle)
    Includes bibliographical references and index.
    Summary: "Describes the uniforms, gear, and weapons used by U.S. and Iraqi forces
during the Iraq War"—Provided by publisher.
    Audience: Grades 4–6.
    ISBN 978-1-4296-7652-6 (library binding)
    1. Iraq War, 2003—Equipment and supplies—Juvenile literature. 2. Military
weapons—United States—History—21st century—Juvenile literature. 3. Military
weapons—Iraq—History—21st century—Juvenile literature. I. Title. II. Series.
DS79.763.T68 2012
956.7044'38—dc23   2011028684

Editorial Credits
Aaron Sautter, editor; Ted Williams, designer; Eric Manske, production specialist

Photo Credits
AP Images: Bilal Hussein, 11 (bottom), Jim MacMillan, cover (soldiers, left); DoD photo, cover
(aircraft), DoD photo by Spc. Michael J. MacLeod, U.S. Army, 29; Getty Images: AFP/Patrick Baz,
4–5; iStockphoto: Craig DeBourbon, 27 (top); Newscom: AFP/Getty Images/Ahmad Al-Rubaye, 13
(top), AFP/Getty Images/Ahmad Al-Rubaye, 15, AFP/Getty Images/USMC/First Bat. Fifth Marines,
14, AFP/Karim Sahib, 11 (top), C3622 Carl Schulze Deutsch Presse Agentur, 17 (middle), Jose
Luis Cuesta Digital Press Photos, 10, KRT/Sylwia Kapuscinski, 19 (top); Shutterstock: Zagibalov
Aleksandr, 9, zimand, 19 (bottom); U.S. Air Force photo by Staff Sgt. Dallas Edwards, 21; U.S. army
photo by Frank Trevino, 23 (top), Sgt. Justin Howe, 27 (bottom), Lance Cpl. Michael J. Yellowhorse,
28, Sgt. Jason Stewart, 13 (bottom), Spc. Jared Eastman, 26 (top), Spc. Teddy Wade, cover (soldier,
right), Staff Sgt. James Selesnick, 12, Staff Sgt. Michael L. Casteel, 8; U.S. Navy Photo, 23 (bottom),
MC1 Eileen Kelly Fors, 22, MC2 Michael Russell, 25 (top); Wikimedia: Department of Defense, 20
(bottom), M62, 17 (top), National War College Military Image Collection, 26 (bottom), PEOSoldier,
16 (both), 17 (bottom), U.S. Air Force photo, 24 (both), U.S. Air Force photo by SRA Greg L.
Davis, 25 (bottom), USMC Gunnery Sgt Mark Olivia, 20 (top); Wikipedia, 18

Artistic Effects
Shutterstock: Ewa Walicka, Fedorov Oleksiy, Gary Paul Lewis, Jules_Kitano, maigi, polispoliviou

Printed in the United States of America in Stevens Point, Wisconsin.
102011   006404WZS12

TABLE OF CONTENTS

⚔ ONE COUNTRY, ⚔ TWO WARS

In 1991 the United States and its allies defeated the Iraqi Army in a fast and furious battle. The source of the conflict was Iraq's **invasion** of its small neighbor Kuwait. After months of threats and troop movements, the U.S.-led nations won Operation Desert Storm in just four days. Iraqi leader Saddam Hussein was forced to pull his forces back to Iraq.

invasion—when a country's military forces enter another country to take it over

But the seeds of war soon began growing again. Hussein had always been interested in gas, biological, and nuclear weapons. He had used such weapons of mass destruction (WMDs) in previous conflicts. After the 1991 war, United Nations weapons inspectors had tried to search Iraq for WMDs. But Hussein continually resisted the inspections. Many world leaders believed Hussein was secretly developing WMDs. By the end of 2002, the United States began calling for another attack on Iraq.

In March 2003, the United States and its allies launched Operation Iraqi Freedom. Hussein's forces were quickly crushed. It looked like it would be another easy victory. U.S. and allied forces stayed in Iraq to provide support as a new government was formed. But many Iraqis did not like the new government. **Insurgents** rose up to fight against it. The allies soon found themselves in a long conflict that would drag on for years.

insurgent—a person who rebels and fights against his or her country's ruling government and those supporting it

5

MAJOR COMBAT

DAY 1: MARCH 20, 2003
- Baghdad is hit with 40 Tomahawk cruise missiles.
- U.S. F-117 Stealth fighter planes drop bombs guided by satellites into Baghdad.
- Iraq sends missiles into Kuwait, but they are intercepted by U.S. Patriot missiles.

DAY 6: MARCH 25, 2003
- The U.S. Army approaches Karbala near Baghdad.

DAY 12: MARCH 31, 2003
- Baghdad is repeatedly bombed.
- British forces prepare to attack Basra, which is still defended by Iraqi troops.

DAY 18: APRIL 6, 2003
- Two to 3,000 Iraqi troops are killed in southern Baghdad.
- British forces continue marching toward Basra.

DAY 27: APRIL 15, 2003
- Iraq's new leaders gather to create a new government.

DAY 43: MAY 1, 2003
- U.S. President George W. Bush announces the end of major combat in Iraq.

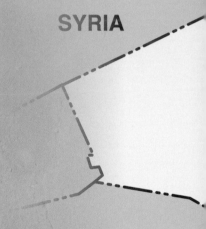

SYRIA

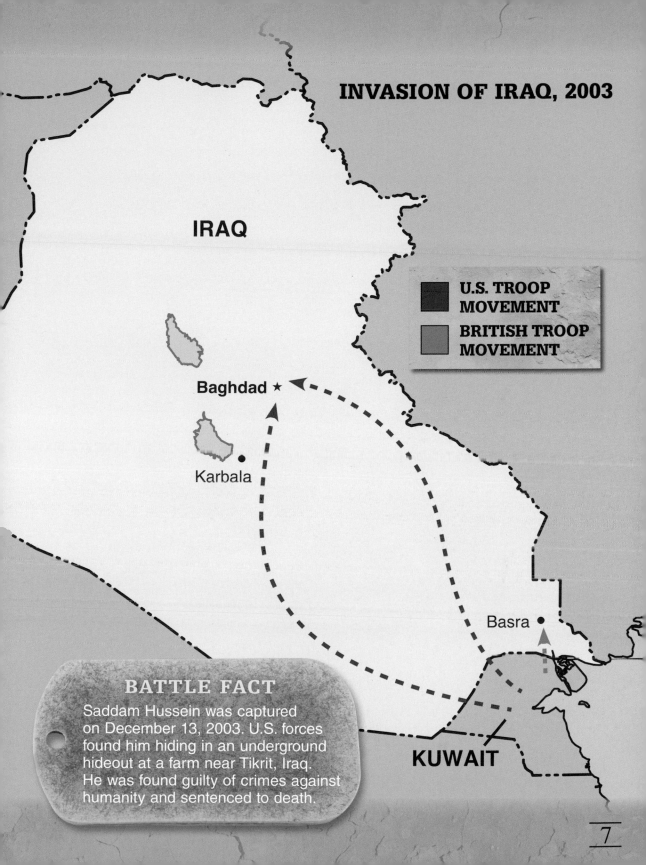

INVASION OF IRAQ, 2003

IRAQ

■	**U.S. TROOP MOVEMENT**
■	**BRITISH TROOP MOVEMENT**

Baghdad ★

Karbala

Basra •

KUWAIT

BATTLE FACT

Saddam Hussein was captured on December 13, 2003. U.S. forces found him hiding in an underground hideout at a farm near Tikrit, Iraq. He was found guilty of crimes against humanity and sentenced to death.

U.S. UNIFORMS

In times of war, soldiers need a variety of reliable weapons, clothing, and gear. In Iraq, the weather can be extreme. During the war, violent sandstorms swirled in temperatures reaching 120 degrees Fahrenheit (49 degrees Celsius) or more. But in spite of the heat, U.S. soldiers had to wear heavy uniforms to protect them from burns, bugs, and bullets.

FLAME-RESISTANT UNIFORMS

Soldiers often risked coming into contact with roadside bombs. To reduce injuries, they wore flame-retardant suits. The material resisted burning for about nine seconds—long enough to jump from a burning vehicle.

COMBAT HELMETS

Padded helmets reduced brain injuries. A face shield was sometimes attached to the helmet to prevent injuries to the face.

DESERT BOOTS

Desert boots had heat-resistant soles. Vents on the boots were eliminated to keep sand and dirt out. Moisture-wicking inserts helped keep soldiers' feet cool and dry.

U.S. STANDARD UNIFORMS

U.S. soldiers wore **camouflage** uniforms with a combination of gray, light green, and tan. The colors allowed soldiers to blend in with inner-city and desert environments.

BATTLE FACT

Soldiers had to closely inspect their boots before putting them on. During the evening, small snakes, scorpions, or poisonous spiders sometimes made their homes inside boots.

camouflage—coloring that helps soldiers blend in with their surroundings

9

IRAQI UNIFORMS

Most Iraqi forces wore standard camouflage clothing. But Saddam Hussein's best troops wore uniforms that set them apart from other soldiers. Meanwhile, insurgent fighters could be anyone, anywhere. They often looked like normal Iraqi citizens.

IRAQI REPUBLICAN GUARD UNIFORMS

The Iraqi Republican Guard were the best soldiers of the Iraqi military. Their uniforms included olive green shirts, jackets, and pants. Members of the guard also wore a red triangle **insignia** on their sleeves.

FEDAYEEN MILITIA

Saddam Hussein's special forces unit was called the Fedayeen Militia. These fighters wore all black uniforms and continued fighting after the regular military had surrendered.

insignia—a badge or design that shows someone's rank or membership in an organization

CEREMONIAL CAPS

An olive green cap was worn by members of the military during ceremonial duties. The hat featured the country's national symbol—a bird bordered with blue stars.

IRAQI HELMETS

Iraqi troops wore combat helmets that looked similar to U.S. helmets from World War II (1939–1945). However, the helmets were made from fiberglass and plastic. They offered little protection against bullets.

INSURGENTS

Insurgent fighters wore regular clothes to avoid calling attention to themselves. To disguise themselves, many wore **kaffiyehs** over their faces.

kaffiyeh—a traditional scarf worn by men in the Middle East

U.S. GEAR

Heat and dust created uncomfortable conditions for soldiers in the desert. The environment was also hard on the troops' gear. The temperatures and sand caused gear to break down. The equipment needed constant repair and replacement.

NIGHT-VISION GOGGLES

Night-vision goggles magnify light from stars and the moon. Pilots used them to see mountains and other obstacles while flying at night in the desert. Ground troops also used night-vision scopes for nighttime missions.

BODY ARMOR

Body armor was made of ceramic plates strong enough to stop bullets and shrapnel. But it was also hot and heavy. Many soldiers took off their armor to prevent heat stroke.

BATTLE FACT

Body armor weighed up to 60 pounds (27 kilograms). Some soldiers said the extra weight kept them from catching quick-footed insurgents.

MODULAR LIGHTWEIGHT LOAD-CARRYING EQUIPMENT

This vest held a variety of equipment, including **ammunition**, grenades, a radio, batteries, and knives. It also included a special suit to protect against chemical and biological attacks.

PROTECTIVE SUNGLASSES

Sunglasses and goggles protected soldiers' eyes from bright sunlight. They also had special foam seals to keep out dust and sand.

THE LAND WARRIOR

The Land Warrior was a mobile computer module attached to a soldier's helmet. It allowed the soldier to track locations, view maps, and review battle plans. Military leaders could send e-mails or talk to anyone wearing the system.

ammunition—bullets and other objects fired from weapons

IRAQI AND INSURGENT GEAR

U.S. forces quickly defeated the official Iraqi military at the beginning of the war. However, insurgent fighters soon began causing problems. Insurgents often used gear and weapons left behind by Iraq's military. They also used farm equipment, tools, and other everyday items to create useful weapons and gear.

BANDOLEERS

Iraqi soldiers often wore bandoleers. A soldier would wear one or two of these cotton belts across his chest and shoulders. The bandoleer carried clips of ammunition used for the soldier's gun.

INSURGENT ADAPTATIONS

Insurgents sometimes turned low-tech objects into useful equipment. Homemade rocket launchers and other weapons could be made from everyday objects like pipes and duct tape.

RECORDING DEVICES

Insurgents didn't have official methods of communication. They carried cameras and video recorders to document their missions instead. They published the images on the Internet to try to scare people and motivate their followers.

RUNNING SHOES

Insurgent fighters and **snipers** usually wore lightweight running shoes instead of heavy boots. Running shoes allowed them to attack quickly and then run away. They were constantly on the move to keep from getting caught.

sniper—a soldier trained to shoot at long-distance targets from a hidden place

U.S. LIGHT WEAPONS

U.S. troops used a variety of light weapons to shoot over short distances and fight in close combat. In the desert environment, light weapons needed to be carefully cleaned and cared for. Some high-tech weapons were sensitive to tiny grains of damaging sand.

M-4 ASSAULT RIFLES

The M-4 weighed about 6 pounds (2.7 kilograms) and used a 30-round magazine. It was a very reliable weapon as long as it was kept clean and well-maintained.

LIGHTWEIGHT SHOTGUNS

Soldiers often used lightweight shotguns to help break through doors. These guns were also known as XM-26 Modular Accessory Shotgun Systems.

M1911-A2 PISTOLS

The original M1911 was a very
successful design that was first used
in World War I (1914–1918). Updated
versions were used in Iraq by both
regular troops and special forces.

M249 SQUAD AUTOMATIC WEAPONS

The M249 was a
portable gas-operated
machine gun. It
was used to support
infantry troops. It
could hit targets at
ranges of up to 2,625
feet (800 meters).

M24 SNIPER WEAPON SYSTEMS

Snipers needed to pass special training to use this rifle. Shooters were
trained to hit targets from 325 to 2,600 feet (100 to 800 m) away using
this system. The weapon used armor-piercing ammunition.

IRAQI AND INSURGENT LIGHT WEAPONS

The traditional Iraqi army was well supplied. However, insurgent fighters had to steal weapons or buy them illegally. Some countries that supported the insurgency also supplied weapons. Insurgents sometimes fixed old weapons and land mines to make them useable again.

PKM MACHINE GUNS

The PKM was a Soviet-made weapon. Its ammunition was held in a detachable barrel. It had dust covers over the loading and ejection windows to keep sand out of the weapon.

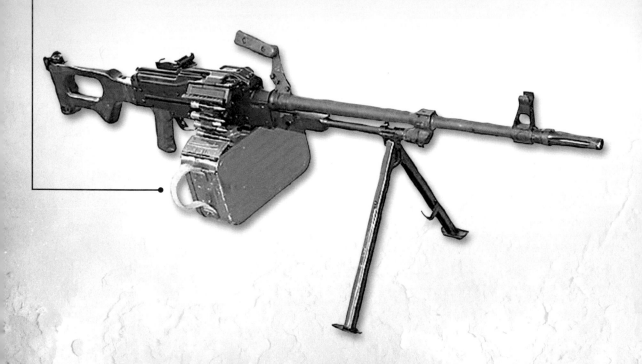

land mine—an explosive triggered by weight; land mines are usually hidden just under the surface of the ground

ROCK THROWING

Insurgents knew that U.S. soldiers would not fire at children. They convinced mobs of young boys to throw rocks at U.S. soldiers. The U.S. troops could be injured if they didn't duck out of the way.

RECYCLED LAND MINES

In the 1980s Iraq was involved in a long war against Iran. During the conflict, Iraqi forces buried millions of land mines throughout the country. Insurgents often dug up these old land mines, repaired them, and used them against U.S. and allied troops.

AKM RIFLES

The Soviet AKM replaced the AK-47 assault rifle of the late 1940s. It was lighter, cheaper, and easier for a soldier to control. It is considered one of the most successful firearms ever produced.

EXPLOSIVES

Explosives are a key part of modern warfare. U.S. forces often used weapons that launched explosives at the enemy. Meanwhile, the insurgents thought of new ways to use explosives. They often littered roads with improvised explosive devices, or IEDs.

U.S. M32 MULTIPLE-SHOT GRENADE LAUNCHERS

The M32 could quickly shoot many grenades with a high degree of accuracy. Quickly firing several grenades was an improvement over single-shot launchers.

IMPROVISED EXPLOSIVE DEVICES (IEDS)

IEDs were made from mortar and artillery pieces. Insurgents often threw these at vehicles or buried them on roads to explode as vehicles traveled over them. Some IEDs could be detonated by a remote control or a cell phone.

U.S. AT-4 ANTI-TANK MISSILE LAUNCHERS

The AT-4 launched guided missiles through a tube. Missiles traveled 600 feet (183 m) per second. They had a maximum range of 6,560 feet (2,000 m). A three-man team was required to carry and set up the weapon. One soldier carried the launcher and tripod while the other two carried the launch tubes.

VEHICLE-BORNE IMPROVISED EXPLOSIVE DEVICES

Insurgents placed some IEDs inside vehicles. They contained explosive charges ranging from 100 to 1,000 pounds (45 to 454 kg). Insurgents often drove these vehicle-based bombs into crowded areas to kill as many people as possible.

SUICIDE BOMB IMPROVISED EXPLOSIVE DEVICES

Some insurgents hid explosive devices under their clothing. They entered a large crowd, and then blew themselves up. Their goal was to cause as much death and chaos as possible.

BATTLE FACT

In 2008 women made up 11 percent of the military units in Iraq and Afghanistan. According to CNN, 180,000 women were in the war zone at that time.

MISSILES AND SMART BOMBS

Heavy weapons range from large guns to **cruise missiles** and vehicles. These deadly weapons were used to take out enemy positions and send enemy troops on the run. Some large weapons were fired from military bases, while others had to be transported to battle sites.

U.S. M777 HOWITZERS

The M777 could be quickly delivered to the battlefield by a helicopter. It had an onboard computer that helped it fire rounds at targets up to 19 miles (31 km) away.

✖ **cruise missile**—a guided missile launched from a ship or aircraft that delivers an explosive warhead

U.S. PATRIOT MISSILE DEFENSE SYSTEMS

Stationed far from battle, the Patriot missile system tracked incoming enemy missiles. A computer guided Patriot missiles toward enemy missiles to shoot them down. However, the Patriot system wasn't always very accurate at hitting incoming missiles.

IRAQI SCUD MISSILE

Iraq had a supply of old Soviet SCUD missiles. The Iraqi military adapted the missiles to fly over longer distances. They also armed the missiles with chemical and biological weapons.

U.S. TOMAHAWK CRUISE MISSILES

Tomahawk missiles could be launched from ships or submarines. They were hard to trace with radar. Tomahawks could hit targets up to 1,550 miles (2,500 km) away.

AIRCRAFT

The United States had an edge in the air war over Iraq. With a bigger budget and better technology, U.S. forces ruled the skies. The United States also improved its ability to target specific military locations and reduce the number of civilian deaths.

U.S. B-2 SPIRIT STEALTH BOMBERS

B-2 Spirit bombers can carry up to 40,000 pounds (18,000 kg) of weapons. They also can carry an advanced cruise missile with a range of up to 1,500 miles (2,414 km).

F-117 NIGHTHAWK STEALTH FIGHTERS

F-117 Nighthawk stealth fighters were officially retired in 2008. The plane allowed pilots to receive new information and redirect a mission from the cockpit. Its advanced attack systems helped U.S. forces fly many successful missions. No Nighthawks were lost in combat during the war.

AH-1W SUPER COBRA ATTACK HELICOPTERS

The Super Cobra is based on the original Huey helicopter that was used in the Vietnam War (1959–1975). Its twin-engine design makes it more stable and safer for pilots.

BATTLE FACT

Specially trained dolphins helped the U.S. Navy clear mines near the port city of Umm Qasr.

U.S. A-10 WARTHOG JETS

The A-10 Warthogs were key weapons in the war's first days. They disrupted and destroyed Saddam Hussein's fleet of tanks. The jets could fly low to support ground troops and hunt down enemy vehicles.

TANKS AND ASSAULT VEHICLES

The United States had more tanks and assault vehicles than Iraq. The vehicles were also more advanced. The Iraqi forces used older tanks from China and the former Soviet Union. Insurgent fighters sometimes used buses and trucks as combat vehicles.

T-72 SOVIET TANKS

Originally designed by the Soviets, the T-72s were the best tanks in the Iraqi military. They were used by the Republican Guard. Regular forces used lesser quality tanks, such as the Chinese-built T-55.

U.S. M2 BRADLEY FIGHTING VEHICLES

The M2 Bradley was designed to carry troops into battle. It was one of the U.S. military's most heavily armored vehicles in the war. It protected soldiers from bullets and explosives.

U.S. LAND ROVERS

Land Rovers were non-military vehicles that were modified for use as light utility vehicles. They could also carry and fire anti-tank weapons. Armor was added to protect the driver and passengers.

U.S. ARMORED HUMVEES

Humvees were one of the U.S. army's main transport vehicles. Up-armored Humvees were fitted with special kits that included armored doors and body panels and bullet-proof glass. The armor helped protect soldiers from enemy fire and IEDs.

MINE RESISTANT AMBUSH PROTECTED VEHICLES (MRAPS)

MRAPs were designed to deflect a blast away from the vehicle when it hit a roadside bomb. It was believed that survival rates were four to five times greater than with armored Humvees.

Every war brings new challenges. New technology is often created to meet those challenges. During the Vietnam War, helicopters became the superstars of the skies. In the Iraq War, computers and other inventions helped protect U.S. troops and defeat the enemy.

THERMAL IMAGING DEVICES

In past wars, soldiers used binoculars to see distant enemies. In Iraq, they often used thermal imaging. This technology allowed soldiers to clearly see what the enemy was doing several miles away—even through darkness and fog.

GLOBAL POSITIONING SYSTEM (GPS)

American drivers often use GPS technology to avoid getting lost on the road. These systems were greatly improved during the Iraq War. U.S. troops could use a GPS with an accuracy range of 10 feet (3 m).

SATELLITE JAMMERS

Iraqi insurgents used low-cost satellite jammers to interfere with U.S. troops' GPS units. However, U.S. forces soon developed anti-jamming technology.

UNMANNED AERIAL VEHICLES (UAVS)

Unmanned aerial vehicles weren't new during the Iraq War. But advancements made them lighter and more effective than before. The vehicles could be tucked into a soldier's backpack and pulled out when needed.

FORCE XXI BATTLE COMMAND BRIGADE-AND-BELOW (FBCB2)

U.S. commanders used the FBCB2 system to track enemies on the battlefield. They could share the enemy's locations with their troops during battles. This advanced computer system took the guesswork out of how, when, and where to fight.

GLOSSARY

ammunition (am-yuh-NI-shuhn)—bullets and other objects that can be fired from weapons

camouflage (KA-muh-flahzh)—coloring on a soldiers' clothing that helps them blend in with their surroundings

cruise missile (KROOZ MISS-uhl)—a guided missile launched from a ship or aircraft that delivers an explosive warhead

insignia (in-SIG-nee-uh)—a badge or design that shows someone's rank or membership in an organization

insurgent (in-SUR-juhnt)—a person who rebels and fights against his or her country's ruling government and those supporting it

invasion (in-VEY-zhuhn)—when a country's military forces enter another country to take it over

kaffiyeh (kuh-FEE-yuh)—a traditional scarf worn by men in the Middle East

land mine (LAND MINE)—an explosive triggered by weight; land mines are usually hidden just under the surface of the ground

sniper (SNY-pur)—a soldier trained to shoot at long-distance targets from a hidden place

READ MORE

Adams, Simon. *The Iraq War.* Secret History. Mankato, Minn.: Arcturus Pub., 2010.

Dougherty, Martin J. *Weapons and Technology.* Modern Warfare. Pleasantville, N.Y.: Gareth Stevens Learning Library, 2010.

Fowler, Will. *The Story of Modern Weapons and Warfare.* A Journey Through History. New York: Rosen Central, 2012.

INTERNET SITES

FactHound offers a safe, fun way to find Internet sites related to this book. All of the sites on FactHound have been researched by our staff.

Here's all you do:

Visit *www.facthound.com*

Type in this code: 9781429676526

Check out projects, games and lots more at
www.capstonekids.com

INDEX